CHRISTMAS HITS
FOR TWO

ISBN 978-1-4950-6918-5

HAL•LEONARD®
CORPORATION
7777 W. BLUEMOUND RD. P.O. BOX 13819 MILWAUKEE, WI 53213

Visit Hal Leonard Online at
www.halleonard.com

CONTENTS

ALL I WANT FOR CHRISTMAS IS YOU

Clarinets

Words and Music by MARIAH CAREY
and WALTER AFANASIEFF

BABY, IT'S COLD OUTSIDE

from the Motion Picture NEPTUNE'S DAUGHTER

CLARINETS

By FRANK LOESSER

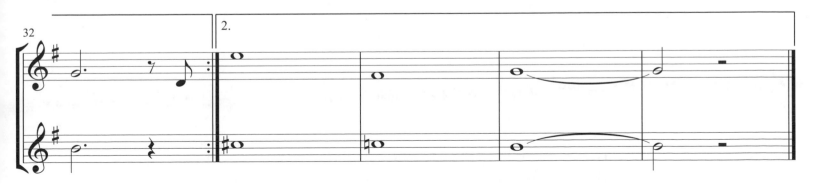

THE CHRISTMAS SONG
(Chestnuts Roasting on an Open Fire)

CLARINETS

Music and Lyric by MEL TORMÉ
and ROBERT WELLS

Moderately slow

THE CHRISTMAS WALTZ

CLARINETS

Words by SAMMY CAHN
Music by JULE STYNE

Moderately fast

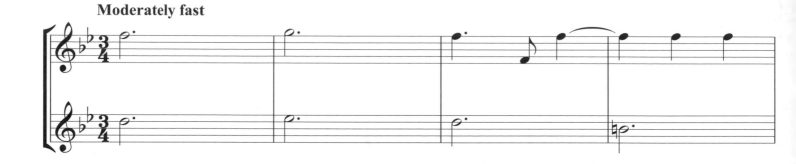

DO YOU HEAR WHAT I HEAR

CLARINETS

Words and Music by NOEL REGNEY
and GLORIA SHAYNE

Moderately

DO YOU WANT TO BUILD A SNOWMAN?

from FROZEN

CLARINETS

Music and Lyrics by KRISTEN ANDERSON-LOPEZ
and ROBERT LOPEZ

Moderately fast

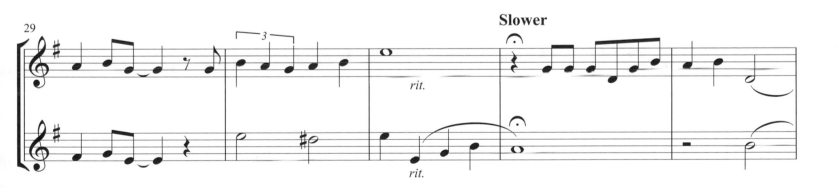

FELIZ NAVIDAD

CLARINETS

Music and Lyrics by
JOSÉ FELICIANO

HAVE YOURSELF A MERRY LITTLE CHRISTMAS

from MEET ME IN ST. LOUIS

CLARINETS

Words and Music by HUGH MARTIN
and RALPH BLANE

Moderately slow

HERE COMES SANTA CLAUS
(Right Down Santa Claus Lane)

CLARINETS

Words and Music by GENE AUTRY
and OAKLEY HALDEMAN

A HOLLY JOLLY CHRISTMAS

CLARINETS

Music and Lyrics by
JOHNNY MARKS

(There's No Place Like)
HOME FOR THE HOLIDAYS

CLARINETS

Words and Music by AL STILLMAN
and ROBERT ALLEN

D.S. al Fine

I'LL BE HOME FOR CHRISTMAS

CLARINETS

Words and Music by KIM GANNON
and WALTER KENT

Moderately

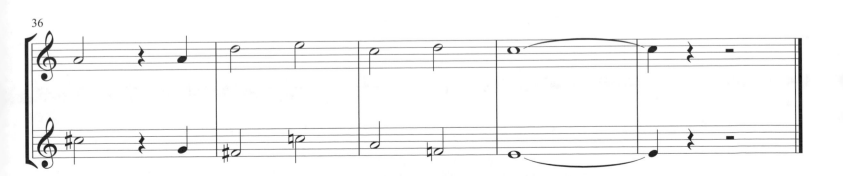

IT'S BEGINNING TO LOOK LIKE CHRISTMAS

CLARINETS

By MEREDITH WILLSON

LET IT SNOW! LET IT SNOW! LET IT SNOW!

CLARINETS

Words by SAMMY CAHN
Music by JULE STYNE

Moderately bright

MARY, DID YOU KNOW?

CLARINETS

Words and Music by MARK LOWRY
and BUDDY GREENE

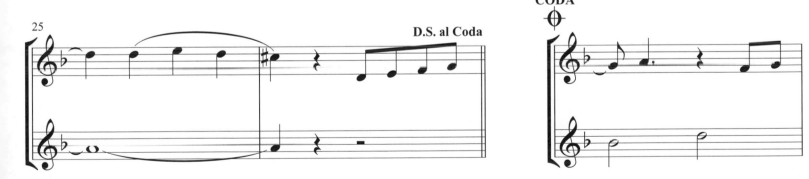

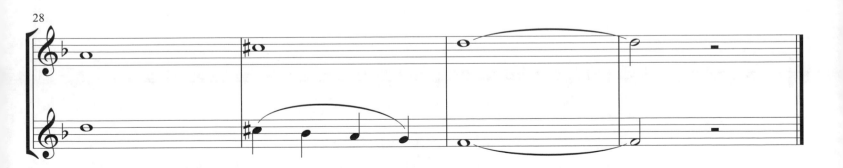

THE MOST WONDERFUL TIME OF THE YEAR

CLARINETS

Words and Music by EDDIE POLA
and GEORGE WYLE

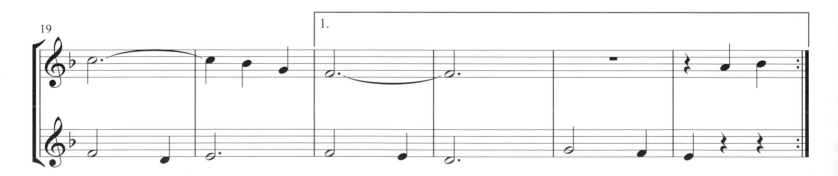

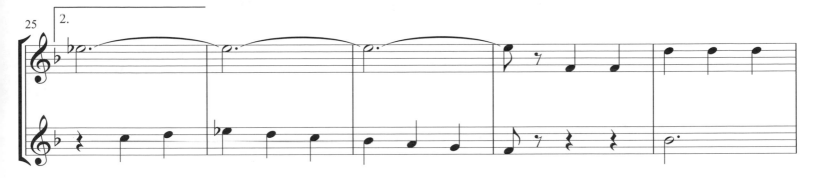

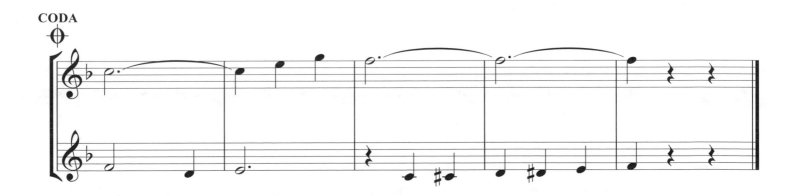

MY FAVORITE THINGS
from THE SOUND OF MUSIC

CLARINETS

Lyrics by OSCAR HAMMERSTEIN II
Music by RICHARD RODGERS

ROCKIN' AROUND THE CHRISTMAS TREE

CLARINETS

Music and Lyrics by
JOHNNY MARKS

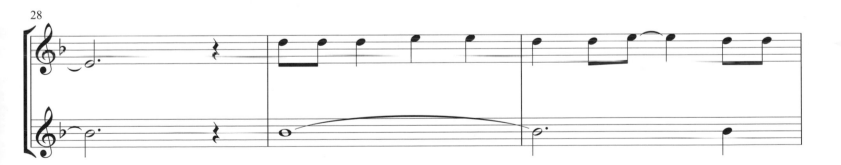

RUDOLPH THE RED-NOSED REINDEER

CLARINETS

Music and Lyrics by
JOHNNY MARKS

SILVER BELLS
from the Paramount Picture THE LEMON DROP KID

CLARINETS

Words and Music by JAY LIVINGSTON
and RAY EVANS

Moderately

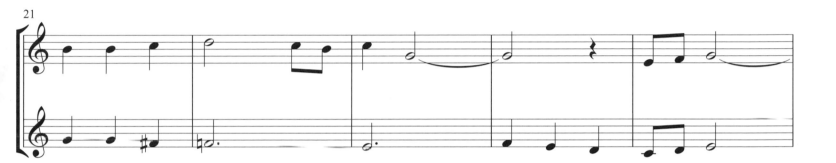

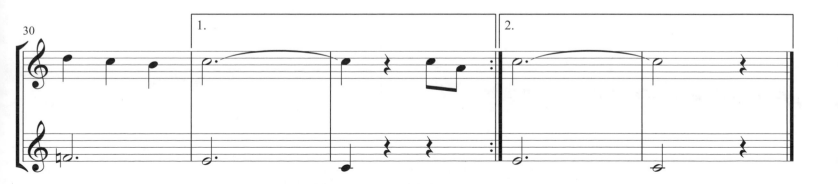

SOMEWHERE IN MY MEMORY

from the Twentieth Century Fox Motion Picture HOME ALONE

CLARINETS

Words by LESLIE BRICUSSE
Music by JOHN WILLIAMS

Moderately

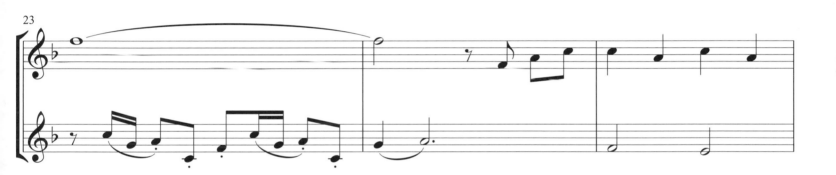

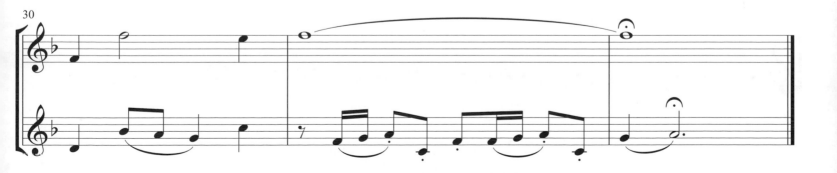

WHITE CHRISTMAS
from the Motion Picture Irving Berlin's HOLIDAY INN

CLARINETS

Words and Music by
IRVING BERLIN

Slowly, in 2

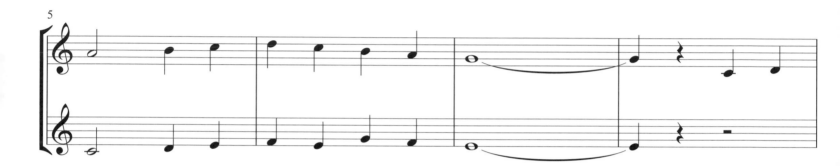

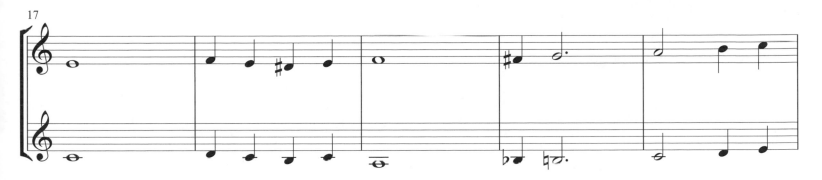

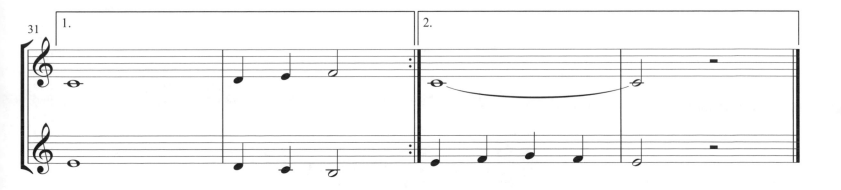

HAL•LEONARD INSTRUMENTAL PLAY-ALONG

Your favorite songs are arranged just for solo instrumentalists with this outstanding series. Each book includes a great full-accompaniment play-along audio so you can sound just like a pro! Check out **www.halleonard.com** to see all the titles available.

Chart Hits

All About That Bass • All of Me • Happy • Radioactive • Roar • Say Something • Shake It Off • A Sky Full of Stars • Someone like You • Stay with Me • Thinking Out Loud • Uptown Funk.

_____ 00146207	Flute	$12.99
_____ 00146208	Clarinet	$12.99
_____ 00146209	Alto Sax	$12.99
_____ 00146210	Tenor Sax	$12.99
_____ 00146211	Trumpet	$12.99
_____ 00146212	Horn	$12.99
_____ 00146213	Trombone	$12.99
_____ 00146214	Violin	$12.99
_____ 00146215	Viola	$12.99
_____ 00146216	Cello	$12.99

Coldplay

Clocks • Every Teardrop Is a Waterfall • Fix You • In My Place • Lost! • Paradise • The Scientist • Speed of Sound • Trouble • Violet Hill • Viva La Vida • Yellow.

_____ 00103337	Flute	$12.99
_____ 00103338	Clarinet	$12.99
_____ 00103339	Alto Sax	$12.99
_____ 00103340	Tenor Sax	$12.99
_____ 00103341	Trumpet	$12.99
_____ 00103342	Horn	$12.99
_____ 00103343	Trombone	$12.99
_____ 00103344	Violin	$12.99
_____ 00103345	Viola	$12.99
_____ 00103346	Cello	$12.99

Disney Greats

Arabian Nights • Hawaiian Roller Coaster Ride • It's a Small World • Look Through My Eyes • Yo Ho (A Pirate's Life for Me) • and more.

_____ 00841934	Flute	$12.99
_____ 00841935	Clarinet	$12.99
_____ 00841936	Alto Sax	$12.99
_____ 00841937	Tenor Sax	$12.95
_____ 00841938	Trumpet	$12.99
_____ 00841939	Horn	$12.95
_____ 00841940	Trombone	$12.95
_____ 00841941	Violin	$12.99
_____ 00841942	Viola	$12.95
_____ 00841943	Cello	$12.99
_____ 00842078	Oboe	$12.99

Great Themes

Bella's Lullaby • Chariots of Fire • Get Smart • Hawaii Five-O Theme • I Love Lucy • The Odd Couple • Spanish Flea • and more.

_____ 00842468	Flute	$12.99
_____ 00842469	Clarinet	$12.99
_____ 00842470	Alto Sax	$12.99
_____ 00842471	Tenor Sax	$12.99
_____ 00842472	Trumpet	$12.99
_____ 00842473	Horn	$12.99
_____ 00842474	Trombone	$12.99
_____ 00842475	Violin	$12.99
_____ 00842476	Viola	$12.99
_____ 00842477	Cello	$12.99

Lennon & McCartney Favorites

All You Need Is Love • A Hard Day's Night • Here, There and Everywhere • Hey Jude • Let It Be • Nowhere Man • Penny Lane • She Loves You • When I'm Sixty-Four • and more.

_____ 00842600	Flute	$12.99
_____ 00842601	Clarinet	$12.99
_____ 00842602	Alto Sax	$12.99
_____ 00842603	Tenor Sax	$12.99
_____ 00842604	Trumpet	$12.99
_____ 00842605	Horn	$12.99
_____ 00842607	Violin	$12.99
_____ 00842608	Viola	$12.99
_____ 00842609	Cello	$12.99

Popular Hits

Breakeven • Fireflies • Halo • Hey, Soul Sister • I Gotta Feeling • I'm Yours • Need You Now • Poker Face • Viva La Vida • You Belong with Me • and more.

_____ 00842511	Flute	$12.99
_____ 00842512	Clarinet	$12.99
_____ 00842513	Alto Sax	$12.99
_____ 00842514	Tenor Sax	$12.99
_____ 00842515	Trumpet	$12.99
_____ 00842516	Horn	$12.99
_____ 00842517	Trombone	$12.99
_____ 00842518	Violin	$12.99
_____ 00842519	Viola	$12.99
_____ 00842520	Cello	$12.99

Songs from Frozen, Tangled and Enchanted

Do You Want to Build a Snowman? • For the First Time in Forever • Happy Working Song • I See the Light • In Summer • Let It Go • Mother Knows Best • That's How You Know • True Love's First Kiss • When Will My Life Begin • and more.

_____ 00126921	Flute	$12.99
_____ 00126922	Clarinet	$12.99
_____ 00126923	Alto Sax	$12.99
_____ 00126924	Tenor Sax	$12.99
_____ 00126925	Trumpet	$12.99
_____ 00126926	Horn	$12.99
_____ 00126927	Trombone	$12.99
_____ 00126928	Violin	$12.99
_____ 00126929	Viola	$12.99
_____ 00126930	Cello	$12.99

Women of Pop

Bad Romance • Jar of Hearts • Mean • My Life Would Suck Without You • Our Song • Rolling in the Deep • Single Ladies (Put a Ring on It) • Teenage Dream • and more.

_____ 00842650	Flute	$12.99
_____ 00842651	Clarinet	$12.99
_____ 00842652	Alto Sax	$12.99
_____ 00842653	Tenor Sax	$12.99
_____ 00842654	Trumpet	$12.99
_____ 00842655	Horn	$12.99
_____ 00842656	Trombone	$12.99
_____ 00842657	Violin	$12.99
_____ 00842658	Viola	$12.99
_____ 00842659	Cello	$12.99

Wicked

As Long As You're Mine • Dancing Through Life • Defying Gravity • For Good • I'm Not That Girl • Popular • The Wizard and I • and more.

_____ 00842236	Flute	$11.95
_____ 00842237	Clarinet	$11.99
_____ 00842238	Alto Saxophone	$11.95
_____ 00842239	Tenor Saxophone	$11.95
_____ 00842240	Trumpet	$11.99
_____ 00842241	Horn	$11.95
_____ 00842242	Trombone	$11.95
_____ 00842243	Violin	$11.99
_____ 00842244	Viola	$11.95
_____ 00842245	Cello	$11.99